CU00847894

Paviland Cave: Ice and Fire

A Commemorative Pamphlet

By Matthew M.C. Smith

Editor: Matthew M. C. Smith
Artist: Rebecca Wainwright

www.blackboughpoetry.com
Twitter: @MatthewMCSmith
Insta: @smithmattpoet
Also on Facebook

First published by Black Bough Poetry in 2023.
Copyright © 2023

LEGAL NOTICE

The right of Matthew M. C. Smith to be identified as the editor of this work has been asserted in accordance with the Copyright, Designs and Patents Act 1988. M.S. Evans reserves the copyright to her work. Typesetting by Matthew M. C. Smith. Artwork by Rebecca Wainwright.

All rights reserved. No part of this book may be reproduced, stored in a retrieval system, or transmitted in any form, or by any means; electronic, mechanical, photocopying, without prior permission from the author and editor. However, short extracts may be quoted on social media. Matthew M. C. Smith has asserted his right under Section 77 of the Copyright, Designs and Patents Act 1988 to be identified as the editor of this work.

Prof. Roberts,

Thanks for requesting this pamphlet! Best, Matthew

This pamphlet commemorates 200 years since the discovery of the 'Red Lady of Paviland'

Ground Plan of the Cave

Drawn by T.Webster from a Sketch by Prof.r Buckland

SECTION OF THE CAVE CALLED GOAT HOLE.
In the Sea Cliffs 1½ Miles West of Swansea.

L.Scharf Lithog.   Printed by C.Hullmandel

About the Author

Matthew M. C. Smith is a writer from Swansea, Wales. He studied for a PhD at the University of Wales, Swansea, on Robert Graves and Celticism. Some of his PhD is published in *The International Journal of Welsh Writing in English*.

Matthew is Best of the Net and Pushcart Prize-nominated. His work can be read in journals, such as *Poetry Wales, The Lonely Crowd, Arachne Press, Icefloe Press, Barren Magazine, Acropolis Journal, Atrium, Seventh Quarry Press, Green Ink, Anti-Heroin Chic, The Storms Journal, Cape Magazine and Bangor Literary Journal*. Matthew won the R.S. Thomas Award for poetry at Gwyl Cybi in 2018.

He runs *Black Bough Poetry, The Silver Branch project* and global poetry platform @TopTweetTuesday on Twitter. He is on Twitter, Facebook and Instagram.

Matthew's collections are *Origin: 21 Poems* (2018) and the recent *The Keeper of the Aeons* with *Broken Spine Arts* (2022)

Website: blackboughpoetry@outlook.com Twitter: @MatthewMCSmith Insta: @smithmattpoet Also on FB

About Rebecca Wainwright - Artist

Rebecca Wainwright is a Welsh architect and illustrator based in London. Website: rebeccaeainwrightart.com Instagram: @wainrightrebs

Photos and artwork:

All photos by Matthew M. C. Smith

Sketch of Paviland Cave from the original excavation. Illustration by T. Webster, based on a sketch by William Buckland.

The Red Man illustration (p2) by Rebecca Wainwright. It was originally published in Black Bough Poetry's 'Deep Time 1'. 'Cavern' is original, for this pamphlet (p17).

Introduction

It is 200 years since William Buckland carried out the first archaeological exploration of Paviland Cave on the coast of Gower, Wales. Buckland discovered a partial skeleton covered in red ochre and burial goods later dated to 33,000 years old, the aurignacian or mesolithic period, although Buckland believed the skeleton to be a Roman prostitute or witch.

In 1923, the discovery of this prehistoric hunter, the enigmatic 'Red Lady of Paviland', led to the artefacts being divided between Wales and Oxford and the skeleton displayed in Oxford Natural History Museum; less focal items and replica items are displayed in museums in Cardiff and Swansea. The Red Lady, now Red Man of Paviland (after scientific testing) lies uprooted hundreds of miles from the isolated, remote Paviland, or Goathole Cave, on the bone-coast of Gower.

In this pamphlet, we travel to a cabinet, one of many other cabinets in a huge room of bones, with the ochre-stained remains taken from the grave, from the land, now housed in a glass-roofed museum in one of the intellectual centres of England and Britain. Visiting a dry room in a museum crowded with different exhibits, I felt bloodless, inert. The Red Man was one of many ancient items divorced from its setting, its resting place. A shrivelling of what should be.

This book brings the bones back to the cave but in mind only. It brings the bones of the hunter back to Wales where they belong. This is our Tutankhamun, only much, much older, vastly older. The hunter is our antiquity, a figurehead to revere, as shown in his burial rites, an ice age ago.

Come with me in mind, in your dreams. One day, the relics will return permanently to Wales and to Swansea, enriching our culture.

Matthew M. C. Smith

January 2023

Note 1: I would like to thank Alan Parry, editor of *Broken Spine*, for agreeing to the reprinting of some material from my collection *The Keeper of Aeons*.

2: In writing this work, I am mindful that this cave is in a very inaccessible location. I hope, therefore, that the imagery I use may allow accessibility for all those readers who would be unable to take this perilous trek. I would not encourage anyone to visit this cave because of risk.

Red King

Royal sun rose;
rise, red king

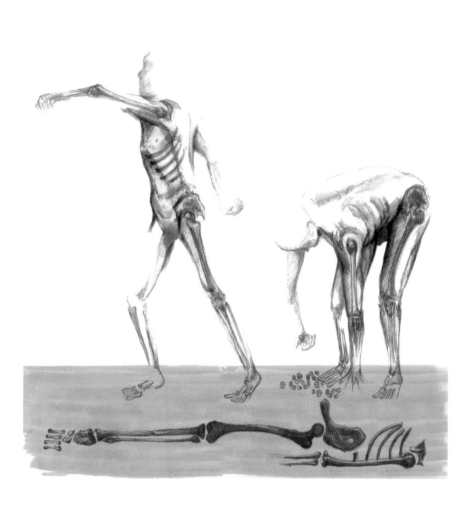

The Climb (Paviland Cave)

The climb on hot rock,
the eastern, high route,
taking its sharp, spiny ridges,
straddling a narrow gorge
above a deep sea-cave's torrent.

The climb, finger-tipping a steep,
diagonal, limestone slab, inching, toeing
a route to a high recess, finally reached, hooked
on, using elbows. A narrow track, baked earth,
yellow-starred gorse; scrub grasses widening to the headland.

I turn into the bay to a rocky platform
seeing out to the ocean's wide brim,
then turn to my right, shin up to a sharper outcrop,
a widening crack in the cliff, 'Goathole Cave'.

Paviland: Ice and Fire

A cave in Gower, site of the burial of a Mesolithic hunter, 33,000 years ago

Fissure of cave. Be in light, shade.
Starve, thirst, slip between worlds.
Tides are time's erasure.

Before The Flood,
the sun and moon commingled
in eclipse of heat and blood.

Dance into flames that lick this chamber,
fall into fathoms before you wake. Kneel
to the lowering of the body in a hollow of rock.

Shadows, faces, eclipsed.

Cover him in sacred ochre with charms for a dead chieftain:
shells of nerite and periwinkle, wands of ivory,
a pendant cone of tusk-bone. Flint tools roughly serrated.

Torches taper. Black smoke-rings. Dark.

Now, is ghost-blue light. Place it all back. Scatter in these rock beds
a wreck of antlers, speckled bones and gnarled-out teeth
from time's migrations, once hoarded, then taken:

Hyenas, bears, rhinoceros. Herds of bison and elk.
Recover the lost skulls of mammoth and the red man. Assemble
his half skeleton. Cover, once more, with ochre.

Through museum's glass, with polished frame felt,
blindly see these shapes shudder through fire and ice.

Fault-Wound

Bone Cave, Gower

In the slew of wide-tide-light, in the boom,
I'm thrust to the shingle-chamber; tip-touch
the braille of rock and heave into the air,
crouched before a fault-wound, an earthen scar.
Step the green shelves – where shadows wind
and kinks of light kick as cupmarks bubble
from a riven roof; lucence of fronds, verdant ferns,
quiver in draughts of the slanting vault. I scratch
cave beds, barely print my feet in dust; a cave-wreck
of Ice Age bones: bison, elk, reindeer, hyena; flints
 worked in haloes of fire. A scattered hoard
before the Flood, before Eden, beneath the blinding
of sky-high ice.

Bone Coast (Paviland)

In late summer, the fields of South Gower are partially visible from the upper coastal path, a circuitous, overgrown, stony route for walkers. Stout drystone walls, thorny hedges and tumbling towers of brambles obscure harvested fields of stubble or rising slopes of curved, cracked earth. The enclosures are edged by hardy trees shaped into petrified, reaching figures by unceasing south-westerly winds. I pass a locked, mud-caked gate, map in hand, observing listless cows grazing. The smell of dung is acrid. In the next field, a tractor criss-crosses the soil. The sky is a perfect blue, with only a fleck of cumulus to the east.

I started the coastal path at the picturesque clifftop village of Rhossili over an hour ago, with its sprawling car park, shoebox-sized shops and acres of sunflowers. I passed groups of visitors with their cameras, ice creams, snacks, rucksacks, walking poles and dogs. I made for the spiny, flat-topped outcrop of 'Worm's Head' taking obligatory photos, readying for the trek. The long spine, the 'Worm' of limestone, resembles a dragon, sunk and cooling in the depths of the glassy sea, which appears still until it breaks as froth on distant sandbanks, pearly outcrops and booms on the shore.

I think about how long it will take to reach the tourist trap of Mumbles, many miles to the east and out of sight. Ahead of me are the monumental headlands, hundreds of feet high, sun-kissed and solemn; pinnacles that need careful navigation before I reach the distant promise of a meal and cold beer in the sweltering evening air. I'm kitted up with food and water, a phone charge booster pack and sunblock.

A series of rocky paths lead through half-cut ferns, gorse and heather to Hunt's Bay. The crowded sunflower fields remain visible from this path, only two stone throws away. About me, the rush of swallows and thrushes that cavort through thickets. Gulls soar and arc on a haze of thermals from sea-caves to summits. I walk above the narrow inlets,

where rockpools gleam green on skin-smooth rocks and dark stacks stand as earth's megaliths. I pass a delicate arrangement of tiny bones like gnarled sticks and a miniature skull socket, swarming with thumb-sized, noisy flies; further along, I slip on a cove's descent and land on jagged stones by a flattened grass-snake with frayed scales on a hollowed-out head.

This is a bone coast. I've been reading various book and internet sites about this area and consider the approximate two hundred years of recorded archaeological explorations; dreamers and theorists that walked as I am, stung by the brush of nettles and brambles, fumbling with maps, alert to discoveries. Using the map, I step up tracks, ascend ancient promontories and ramble through prehistoric earthworks covered with bushes that carousel with butterflies and thrum with crickets.

I head for Paviland Cave, the focus of this sole expedition. I have no sense of where it is and what it really looks like. I track the shape of the headlands on the map and after miles of hesitance, I eventually see the jutting Paviland coastline. Paviland, that lone place; the site of the oldest known burial in Europe, a prehistoric shrine in a cavern also known as 'Goathole Cave'. I am mindful of its reputation as a place difficult to get to. Its isolation and inaccessibility resulted in it being untouched for tens of thousands of years. Eventually, after passing the conspicuous headland on the inland pathway, I come to a sloping causeway of rocks, cascading down to the sea in a narrow valley. I soon observe the natural platform of rock, accessed by a sloping face to be climbed on a diagonal with ample holds and cracks. The route is not particularly difficult but it is unnerving; the sea-cave deafeningly churns below and some of the cracks are hairline. What lies above and beyond?

Unless the tide is extremely low, the only route to Paviland Cave without ropes is the 'high' pathway and when ascended, the dazzling vista of the bay unexpectedly opens out. I stand utterly alone under the blistering glare of noon with the vast sea metres below, flowing out to the Bristol Channel. To the right, the bleached limestone cliffs rise high to the summit. A cave mouth is discernible, then unmistakable. Over sharp rocks, the entrance of the gaping mouth is reached. I walk into the fissure, seeing its chimney-like chamber metres above, and peer into the half-light noting the series of stony beds and cave floor troughs that have been repeatedly excavated. This is a place of revelation.

About 33,000 years ago, a man was buried here, ceremonially covered in red ochre with a trove of primitive grave goods: a pendant made from part of a mammoth tusk; bored periwinkle shells and ivory 'wands' discovered in loose piles, which are likely to have been decorative; a serrated harpoon blade pulled out from this penetrated layer. In the various layers excavated in this burial site, and in other caves around the coast, the bones of extinct animals and species long-gone from this climate have been uncovered – cave lions, bears, Irish elk, bison, rhinoceros, hyena and mammoth, along with thousands of rudimentary flints worked by ancient people.

As I sit in the cave, sipping water carelessly from a clear flask, skin prickling with heat and nettle rashes, I see water drops from my chin dry on the stones between my feet. I will leave almost nothing here, barely a mark or a turned stone. I recall that some of the discoveries from the stony bed I crouch on are on display in Swansea and Cardiff museums though I have not seen them for years. The partial skeleton and more significant remnants, however, are far away in Oxford, taken there by William Buckland, the archaeologist and friend to the Talbot family of Penrice Castle, who requested he investigate after two excavations in 1822 had uncovered bones. Buckland descended from the clifftop on a rope. These shadows in their tweed clothes, bonnets, hats and petticoats run through my mind and seem to pass in air, flowing over the contours of the cave. Then there is stillness, once more, and a sense of loss spiralling, descending slowly within me, a gnawing emptiness. This is the cave; the place I sought. I will leave whatever sanctity remains. I have reverence to whatever is left of the tomb of the red king.

Nothing we claim, nothing we take, is ever left sacred. We search for, stumble on relics, then disinter, rupture, index, box, move, display. We eat the heart out of the earth, remove and slay the union of artefact and place. We replace with banal; the air-conditioned room, keeping it all 'safe'. Here lay the body, here under my feet – an Alexander, Xerxes, Tutankhamun of Wales; only older, so much older. Ice Ages and aeons past and impossible to fully grasp. I think about our relics, so many that lie far away; we the people in the west, dispossessed. It is others' gold.

I return. I walk. The sun beats. Shadow runs behind me and as I turn, flies glow in the dazzle of midday fire.

Facing the Red Man

At Oxford Natural History Museum

It's a drain
to see these pinned up relics
from my far-off, lonely bone coast
with its shelter carved above the water-plane;
here in this one, watched over, polished case,
in this gallery with a glass-roofed hall –

the Red Man.

I feel a drain - this disconnection of bone and bed,
as I press my nose to glass in this vault,
leaning inwards, skull towards skeleton,
eyeballs to ochre-red frame of blades and know it, all of it,
as more than headless and dispossessed.

Buckland found and took these pieces.
Somewhere, there's a tusk of a mammoth,
boon from the burial. Someone's secret?

And all the time it has taken, to get to this point,
all the aeons, it is taken from us.

Ogof Coygan (Coygan Cave)

A prehistoric cave near Laugharne, West Wales, where Neanderthal (stone) hand axes were discovered in an ancient hyena den with other prehistoric remains. The was destroyed in 1964 by a mining company. One of the axes is in Cardiff museum.

The hoard: hand axes, triangular stones, filling the palm-grip that cleave, cut, scrape, crack and smash, used to pummel by shadowy, kneeling figures far, far back, silhouetted against the source of light. Close to these tools remnants of hyena teeth lay on curved, decayed, scimitar-like jawbones. They are scraped and brushed out of layers of stone and dust and cleaned in the cavern of rock at Coygan Quarry, a mile from the coast. Remains too of rhinoceros and bison, common with other bone caves on the Welsh coast.

The salvage is held by gloved fingers and placed under a spotlight; it is placed, sealed, studied, under print-rings of tip-smeared glass in the expanse of a room with wooden, Victorian floor-boards that spring and creak; a shrine of bone and stone, encased for the intermittent procession of gazers. He sees, she imagines; they peer up close.

I've seen these relics and stumbled on the fate of the cave late one night, while reading, amazed that a mining company could destroy this site with its Neanderthal deposits; the paradox of human destruction versus quiet veneration.

In moments alone, I can separate, move, travel. With intense focus, light blurs; I turn to the vision inwards, losing presence. I bound, dive, plummet. I walk through a raven glade to the edge feeling blood and pulse beat, coursing through the body. The fence is broken. I walk over undulations of wire to pebble beds at the green edge.

The unveiling: I stand at a distance from the vertiginous rock. It is there now. I stand in a grit bed at the quarry base and take the rise to uneven, carved slopes, trekking dust levels strewn with earth's karst; boulders, regoliths and chundered rock. The buttressed cliffs and low cavern's mouth meet the new sun; tilted contours of the rock-face shine all hues; the camera shoots an image of the cave dead-centre; the image is imprisoned in flame, a bright ring flecked with technicolour.

Neanderthal place, hyena den, mouth of bones. Open-cast quarry.

Earth blast, dynamite quake, seismic sound, sonic boom.

Diggers excoriate ruins in dust-fog. Too late.

When everything clears, eyes conjure images that twist in the spectrum. The cave in the air in the mind is glass, a mirror, recreated with hands, fingers, eyes; the ecstasy of grey matter seeing right through, searching towards its fall into darkness; a glory of walls spinning ever-back. It is a castle, a many-faced crystal, a Caer Sidi of imagination, opened to light.

The pounding on flesh, rock and earth. The skeletal, rust-burnished excavators. The low murmur of blood.

The turning of the lock. Measured footsteps in the hall. Streams of evening sunlight. The parched silence of a room with cabinets.

Famous Bones Come Home

The Paviland Cave relics return to Swansea from Oxford in 2058,
more than two hundred and thirty-five years after it being
deemed that Swansea was not suitable to house such a find.

The sacred relics are driven back in padded casing,
they slightly shake at the rear of the secure van –
micro-vibrations; one man stays in the front,
as the other takes a pee at the service station.
The government minister in a glass-wooden-metal
building in Cardiff Bay is on the phone speaking in Welsh
with the Minister of Public Works; they have the Rugby
Captain cutting the ribbon in three days' time. All week,
professors, archaeologists, historians, nationalists and
journalists have been recasting the narrative, cutting it
from coal, copper, mines, druids, harps and heroic failure.
They are calling it our 'Elgin Marbles' and, once again, we
are digging ourselves into the land; getting entrenched
is an ecstatic connection. Now ice and hunters and deep time
across a chilly landscape and the oldest human burial in Europe, an
Ice Age hunter, hidden in a rock shelter and in Gower, yes Gower.
All week, the news has told of the 'Lady' and its red shift to
'Man' and of famous bones coming home; once imagined
as a witch, or prostitute, now turned fur-clad hunter.
They are calling this our 'Tutankhamun', and the explorers
are making their way to Cymru through the skies. They've
closed Paviland Bay with hazard tape – a bad accident –
where a wild-haired, ill-equipped, over-zealous octogenarian
slipped from a limestone crag and broke a lot of bones. He was
airlifted away, breathing in gas, touch and go in a Welsh
hospital because, this time, we could do it in Wales,
we could sort out bones. Yet this hunter, this cavern-bound
pilgrim, kept his head and ten weeks later limped in
to the *Oxford Natural History Museum Wing* of Swansea
Museum, throwing his crutches and bounded towards the

augmented-reality exhibition full of tourists, where the
cased remains lay on silver felt: a neck pendant made of tusk,
its wands of ivory, decorative shells of nerite and periwinkle,
adorned with Mesolithic bling. He sank to his knees, clasping
his hands as surround-sound mammoths roared.

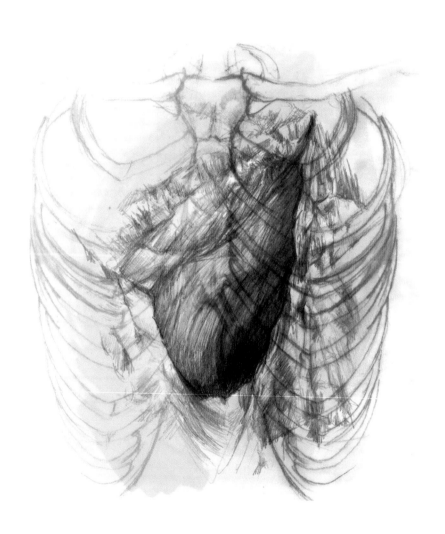

Other Books by Black Bough Poetry/ Matthew M. C. Smith, available online:

Deep Time, volume 1 – 2020

Deep Time, volume 2 - 2020

Christmas-Winter - 2020-21

Under Photon Crowns: Selected Writing of Dai Fry - 2021

Dark Confessions - 2021

Freedom-Rapture – 2021

Christmas-Winter – 2021-2022

Afterfeather - Black Bough Summer edition 2020
(guest edited by Briony Collins)

Sun-Tipped Pillars of Our Hearts: the Dai Fry Award for Mystical Poetry anthology –
Autumn 2022

'Duet of Ghosts': after poems - 2022
(guest edited by Jen Feroze)

Nights on the Line by M.S. Evans

The Keeper of Aeons by Matthew M. C. Smith - Broken Spine Arts – Autumn 2022.

Christmas-Winter – 2022-23

Paviland Cave: Fire and Ice. A Commemorative Pamphlet., by Matthew M. C. Smith

Forthcoming:

Black Bough Poetry – Tutankhamun edition (centenary) - 2023

Black Bough Poetry – T.S. Eliot's 'The Wasteland' edition (centenary) - 2023

Poetry collections by Matt Gilbert, Sarah Connor, Rachel Deering and Andy MacGregor

Printed in Great Britain
by Amazon

19042428R00016